WHEN YOUR
CHRISTIANITY
RENDERS YOU
INEFFECTIVE

RECLAIMING GOD'S INTENTION

FOR HIS CHURCH AND HIS PEOPLE

Derrick A. Smith

WHEN YOUR CHRISTIANITY RENDERS YOU INEFFECTIVE

Copyright © 2016 by Derrick A. Smith.

For information or booking contact :

Soul Reconstruction

214-450-8397

Email : dsmith@soulreconstruction.com

http://www.soulreconstruction.com

Book and Cover design by Janiel Jkheck

Book Formatting by Derek Murphy @Creativindie

Book Editing by Salena Smith

ISBN-13: 978-0998361208

ISBN-10: 0998361208

First Edition: November 2016

10 9 8 7 6 5 4 3 2 1

CONTENTS

Introduction

SO YOU SAY YOU'RE A CHRISTIAN, but is that really saying a lot these days? How do people respond to you when you openly say this? Do they open up their doors and welcome you with open arms, or do they shut you out? Do they look at you with suspicion as if you can't be trusted? Do they hold tightly to their wallet or purses for fear that you will beg or even steal from them? Sadly, more and more, this is becoming the prevailing perception of Christians.

There was once a time in this country when saying you were a Christian meant something. Professing to be a Christian meant that you were trustworthy and dependable. Christian pastors were revered and respected in the community. People would refuse to curse in the presence of a Christian. They would put out their cigarette or put up their wine if a pastor was nearby. They were mindful of the things they said and did in the presence of children. Morality was not just a notion, but rather a way of life. Being a Christian was a mark of distinction that people aspired to be. What happened to this distinction? How did the lines get blurred?

Chapter 16 of the book of Acts tells a story about Paul and Silas preaching in Thyatira where they encountered a young slave girl who had a spirit of divination. Her masters used her to tell fortunes for their profit. Whenever Paul and Silas would preach, the girl would affirm their words by telling the people, "Listen to these men. They show you the way to God." Now, one would assume that since these men were preaching the truth about Christ and His Kingdom that her amen would be welcomed support, and it appeared to be initially. This went on for a couple of days, but one day, finally the Apostle Paul became troubled in his spirit and discerned that this was a demon and immediately cast it out of the girl. You might ask yourself, why was the girl's support of Paul's message such a problem? She never disputed their words, as you would assume the devil would, being that Satan opposes everything God stands for. Take into consideration that she was known by the people for practicing divination, a dark art. So her support of the apostles' message could be mistaken as an alliance between herself and Paul, and the people would discount their message, diluting the effect of the word on the hearts and minds of the people.

One of the greatest misconceptions about the contrast between Christ and Satan is that everything is black and white. We believe the schemes of the devil are clearly pointed out. They are not! Evil is not always so easily identified like in the old western movies where the bad guy wore black and the good guy wore white. Satan specializes in the counterfeit, and as you know, counterfeits aren't worth their weight unless they can fool even the trained eye.

I recall when I was in grade school, the local police would visit all the area schools with the *Say No to Drugs* campaign. They would tell the kids to watch out for drug dealers, and the characters they would present as drug dealers were people no child would normally entertain. They would act out a scene where this suspicious character would walk up to a random kid and offer him or her drugs, and naturally the kid would say NO! The dealer would ask a few more times to suggest persistence and every time the kid would passionately refuse until the dealer gave up and went on about his business.

Later in life, I discovered that this is not how it happens at all. People who are introduced to drugs are usually introduced to them by someone they are close to and have a relationship with. It's their friend who happens to have access to drugs, or maybe a beloved family member whom they admire, who first exposes them to it and eventually gives them their first taste of marijuana, cocaine, or alcohol. It's not the street thug drug dealer as most people suspect, since most dealers use discretion and prefer not to advertise their products.

Also, the introduction usually takes place when you are very vulnerable and are at an emotional low point in your life. Such is the case with most people who make the decision to accept Christ as their savior. Life has presented challenges that you are not emotionally equipped to deal with, and you are trying to endure the preverbal "beat-down" from all of its stresses and circumstances. Where this does present a wonderful opportunity for Christ to come in and change your life, Satan is also aware of your condition and will use your vulnerable state to his advantage as well. He even came to temp Christ at a very weak moment when He was in the wilderness, using even God's word to try to pull Him off course from completing His God-given assignment. We can't believe for a minute that this method of Satan's ended with Christ in the wilderness. He is still pulling the same stunts today.

In John 10:10, Jesus tells us, "The thief comes only to steal and kill and destroy; I have come that you may have life, and have it to the full" (NIV). To this day, Satan is still robbing us of the full life that Christ came to give us. He is stealing our dreams, killing our hope, and destroying our ability to carry out our God-given purpose in the earth. He has done an outstanding job at rendering us ineffective, both as individuals and the church as a whole. We are the body of Christ, and as a body is made up of many different smaller parts, so is Christ's body. In order to infect your whole body, only a small part has to be exposed to the infection first. Eventually, that infection will spread and weaken the entire body. This has become the case with the Christian church today. Satan has infected us with subtle lies and misconceptions that we as a body have adopted as standard practices, rules, and doctrines. The effects, whereas not very immediate, have slowly began to deteriorate the church and is seriously affecting the health of the body.

The church is being robbed of its power and authority. We look at the power of the early church and marvel at the wonderful things they accomplished. Jesus Christ overcame the world, yet we seem to keep falling victim to its systems and appear to be at its mercy. What happened to that effective draw of converts by the thousands as the gospel of the Kingdom and Christ was being preached by the apostles? What happened to the signs and wonders and "greater works" Christ said that we would do? Why aren't things measuring up to what God said in His word? Is God no longer fulfilling His promises? Is the power that was available to the early church no longer available to the church today? If He is the same yesterday, today, and forever, what has changed?

I remember a catchy phrase that was popular in the church recently that said "It's not about religion. It's about relationship!" Although very true, we still seem to settle for religion, and if religion was not God's intention, why do we continue in it and pass on the relationship? Has the Christian church settled for just a position in the ranks of the world's major religions? Is this religion called Christianity accomplishing God's purposes in the earth?

In this book, we will examine a few of the unwritten rules of Christianity to see if they measure up to God's standards and intentions. We will also take a look at some of the beliefs and practices within modern Christianity that hinder us from reaching our potential as children of God. This book will address the subtle lies Satan has allowed us to adopt into our lives. By the end, it is my desire that we will be more equipped to dismiss the things that are causing us to be ineffective.

CHAPTER 1

BROKE CHURCH, BROKEN PEOPLE

THERE IS NO MISTAKING THE FACT that you can find a church in almost any neighborhood in America. In some cities and towns, it is not uncommon to find three or four churches within a two mile radius. The ironic thing is that this occurs mostly in the poorest neighborhoods of a city.

Why is this ironic? Well, when you look at the fact that God owns everything, and riches and glory are attributed to His name, yet the institution that represents Him is located in the poorest neighborhoods. Now I know you're probably saying, "I don't see the irony here," and you're right about that. It makes sense for Christ to be in the places where He is most needed. The irony comes when you look at how long those churches have been there with no improvement in the conditions of the area. There is a diminishing sense of community, crime continues to increase, and teenage pregnancy (which is a problem it seems no one addresses anymore) becomes an expected occurrence. Drug abuse is a method of coping with all the craziness these neighborhoods hold. Now here's the most ironic thing of all...the drug of choice for a lot of the people in these communities is the Sunday morning message.

How in the world could a Sunday morning message be a drug? Well, ask yourself this, why do people use drugs? Is it not to find a temporary escape from the stress and worry brought on by trying to cope with the problems a person is experiencing? This is the same thing that occurs when Sunday after Sunday people pack the pews to listen to a message that gives them a rush of emotions, triggers a euphoric sensation, and can rival any blunt they could smoke. But after the benediction is given they return home to the same hopeless situations they were enduring all along.

This is the danger of preaching messages that entertain people rather than empower them. Sermons that entertain make emotion the priority and devalues true teaching that could provoke real transformation in the heart of congregants. There are individuals in some churches who honestly believe the preacher hasn't begun to preach until he has gone into his "hoop". People will even go as far as tuning a preacher out that doesn't give them the show they're looking for; their proverbial "hit", if you will.

There are churches in America that are turning out more junkies than any of the drug dealers plaguing our cities. Living life in lack is quite difficult, and life's challenges are a constant reminder of how horrible it feels to not have the things you need. I am not making excuses, but rather stating a fact, and people in these situations need an escape, at least mentally, even if it's for a brief moment. The problem is that getting high will never solve any problem. So when you come down, returning to those problems is inevitable. This influences people to continue chasing that high. People need sound teaching that will give them what they need to actually go out and do something about those problems.

Don't get me wrong, emotional messages that entertain are good to listen to, but they don't promote real change. I firmly believe that you cannot truly commit your whole life to Christ and His principles and remain the same. God is more concerned with our character than our situation because He knows that if you change a man's character, you can change his circumstances. This is what God is referring to when He says He wants us to be conformed to the image of Christ. The image of Christ is not a physical image. It is the character of Christ, and make no mistake, God is in the character-building business, even more so than the blessing business or the miracle-working business. The latter two of these is the focus of most entertaining messages. It's the same thing as consuming junk food while avoiding what's healthy. It continues to create unhealthy saints, which creates unhealthy churches.

Another danger of preaching junk messages is that it gives people a false sense of who God is. He is not an irresponsible parent. He's not going to cave in and give you what you want because you kick, scream, cry, and snot all over yourself and every usher in the building. The Parent of the Year award will never be given to a father or mother willing to give their eight-year-old the keys to their car with the intent to drive. A loving parent, out of concern for the child's life and well-being, will wait on that child to mature to the point where they are knowledgeable and responsible enough to handle such a huge responsibility. Often, people are not being fed the things that will promote healthy growth and maturity, yet they wonder why they are not experiencing the blessings of God. It is an act of mercy on God's part to withhold the things from us that He knows will destroy us.

"God does not give you what you pray for. He only gives you what you can manage." - Dr. Myles Munroe

Psalm 84:11 says, "no good thing will He withhold from them that walk uprightly." (KJV). No baby starts off walking upright. It's only through a process of growth and change that a child is able to do so. Growth in Christ is not like growing physically. It doesn't just naturally happen. It is forced through an act of your will as you seek God and His truth. You don't grow in Christ by just sitting in a church, feeding yourself only the things you want to hear, and certainly not by only opening your bible once or twice a week when you go to church. It's a result of you learning the complete truth of His word and applying it to your life. This is why real parents would not allow their kids to eat dessert before they had their dinner. They always said it would "spoil your appetite." Unfortunately, some of us do not have an appetite for sound teaching based on God's principles.

We need to develop a healthy appetite for God's word again,

but how do we do this? We must give people the truth, the whole truth, and nothing but the truth. For instance, God's promises are conditional. Unhealthy messages focus on the promises, but put little or no emphasis on the conditions. The conditions must be fulfilled before you can experience the promises. The promises will get a congregation on their feet clapping and cheering! You're liable to get some shouting and dancing along with it. The conditions will make you sit and listen and consider whether you are able to meet them, and if you're really willing to do what's necessary to experience the promises.

Once, Jesus had a large crowd following Him, and knowing that many of them were doing so purely for what they could get from Him; He turned and addressed them saying...

"If anyone comes to me and does not hate father and mother, wife and children, brothers and sisters—yes, even their own life— such a person cannot be my disciple. And whoever does not carry their cross and follow me cannot be my disciple. "Suppose one of you wants to build a tower. Won't you first sit down and estimate the cost to see if you have enough money to complete it? For if you lay the foundation and are not able to finish it, everyone who sees it will ridicule you, saying, 'This person began to build and wasn't able to finish.' "Or suppose a king is about to go to war against another king. Won't he first sit down and consider whether he is able with ten thousand men to oppose the one coming against him with twenty thousand? If he is not able, he will send a delegation while the other is still a long way off and

will ask for terms of peace. In the same way, those of you who do not give up everything you have cannot be my disciples. (Luke 14:26-33 NIV)

God knows our true intentions. I cringe when I hear people say, "God knows my heart", a phrase often used as a cop-out for some mistake someone has made. This is a very true statement indeed, but one that should cause you to be more concerned than careless. It means you can never pull a fast one on Him because He knows your true motives. That's why we can never fake our way into a blessing from God. The show we put on is purely for the people watching, but it has become customary in the Christian church to keep up this charade. I know what you're saying, "Who are you to say if someone is being fake or not?" Consider the words of King Jesus in Luke 6:43-44...

"No good tree bears bad fruit, nor does a bad tree bear good fruit. Each tree is recognized by its own fruit. People do not pick figs from thornbushes, or grapes from briers." (Luke 6:43-44 NIV)

The problem is that sermons of no substance have made living for Christ sound so easy when the truth of the matter is if it were easy, everyone would do it! Jesus said that broad is the way that leads to destruction, narrow is the way that leads to life, and there are few that find it. No matter how many times in His word God warns us of the challenges associated with living for Him, we still fail to heed his warning. We allow ourselves to be fooled into thinking that once I give my life to Christ all I have to do is kick my feet up and let Him do everything for me.

A lot of us have adopted this doctrine where if I face anything difficult, it's an attack of the enemy, or we feel like God has abandoned us or let us down. Dr. Myles Munroe said that "God will never trust what He hasn't tested." With that in mind, how do you think these tests come? They come in challenges and trials! When Jesus was about to begin His earthly ministry, He went to John the Baptist to be baptized. We read about how when He came up out of the water, the heavens opened and the Holy Spirit descended on Him like a dove, and God spoke from heaven and said "This is my beloved son in whom I'm well pleased." For the sake of this point, let say that this is the equivalent of one of those powerful worship services you attended where it was prophesied to you that you are going to do and have great things! You fall all out on the floor, get lint in your hair, break out into your Holy Ghost dance and begin praising God like a wild person! The prophet may have even told you to run around the sanctuary or sow a seed to claim this word, so you sprint around the place (asthma and all) and reach deep in your pocket to pull out your best seed (you know the one you were going to use to get your hair done or get 'dem new J's) and put it in the offering. Everything's ready now, right? You can just step into your prosperity now, right?

Consider this...what was the first thing that happened to Jesus after He was baptized? The Spirit, not Satan, drove Him into the wilderness TO BE TESTED! If even Jesus Christ had to be tested, how on earth would you think you were exempt? And who did God allow to tempt Him? Yes! The devil! How are you ever going to truly realize the truth of greater is He that is in you than he who is in the world if you never allow yourself to be tested? How are you ever going to be more than a conqueror if you never accept a challenge? True courage manifests in the face of fear.

Any teaching or doctrine that leads someone to believe that every difficult situation they encounter or hardship they endure is from the devil is setting them up for failure. It's this kind of doctrine that keeps people bound and afraid to progress or move out of their situation, no matter how horrible their current one is. We use phrases like "I'm just waiting on God" or "All in God's timing" and God has been waiting on us for years. The time is now! You knew you heard Him the first time when that still, small voice told you to "Get up and do something!" The fact that God allowed it is evidence that you can overcome it. So ask yourself, "What am I really waiting on?"

When God speaks and gives a command, the time is always now. His word says "NOW" faith is the substance of things hoped for and evidence of things not seen. It didn't say "THEN" faith or even "LATER" faith, but rather "NOW" faith. Faith is the currency by which we do business with God. Have you ever missed out on a great investment opportunity or a nice purchase because you didn't have the money "NOW", at that moment, and the opportunity passed you by? That's what it's like when we don't have the faith to move on God's word right when He sends it. As the writer in the third chapter of Hebrews states...

"While it is said, Today if ye will hear his voice, harden not your hearts, as in the provocation. For some, when they had heard, did provoke: howbeit not all that came out of Egypt by Moses. But with whom was he grieved forty years? Was it not with them that had sinned, whose carcases fell in the wilderness? And to whom sware he that they should not enter into his rest, but to them that believed not? So we see that they could not enter in because of unbelief." (Hebrews 3:15-19 KJV)

If the messages that come from the pulpit at your church only deal with what God can and will do for you, and never emphasize what your responsibility is to Him and His people, you're in the wrong church. We spend so much time wondering if we can trust God when the bigger question is always can He trust us. And the second is like unto the first...can we trust ourselves? If I loan you my car, who has the greater burden of trust? I do! The earth is the Lord's and the fullness thereof. That means He owns everything. So why do we worry so much about if He can be trusted? Our greatest concern should be whether or not we are trustworthy. What I've found in my own life is that the more of my life and myself that I committed to God and His ways, the more He entrusted into my care.

The one person God can trust is Himself. Why do you think He put so much effort into conforming us into the image of His

Son? The image of Christ is not a physical image! His image is His character and likeness or behavior. Once we adopt the character of the King, He can trust us.

The fallen nature of man is too untrustworthy. In the seventh chapter of Romans, the Apostle Paul talks about this struggle.

"So the trouble is not with the law, for it is spiritual and good. The trouble is with me, for I am all too human, a slave to sin. I don't really understand myself, for I want to do what is right, but I don't do it. Instead, I do what I hate. But if I know that what I am doing is wrong, this shows that I agree that the law is good. So I am not the one doing wrong; it is sin living in me that does it. And I know that nothing good lives in me, that is, in my sinful nature. I want to do what is right, but I can't. I want to do what is good, but I don't. I don't want to do what is wrong, but I do it anyway. But if I do what I don't want to do, I am not really the one doing wrong; it is sin living in me that does it. I have discovered this principle of life—that when I want to do what is right, I inevitably do what is wrong. I love God's law with all my heart. But there is another power within me that is at war with my mind. This power makes me a slave to the sin that is still within me. Oh, what a miserable person I am! Who will free me from this life that is dominated by sin and death? Thank God! The answer is in Jesus Christ our Lord. So you see how it is: In my mind I really want to obey God's law, but because of my sinful nature I am a slave to sin." (Romans 7:14-25 NLT)

Paul gave the hope for this condition in the eighth chapter of Romans.

"But you are not controlled by your sinful nature. You are controlled by the Spirit if you have the Spirit of God living in you. (And remember that those who do not have the Spirit of Christ living in them do not belong to him at all.) And Christ lives within you, so even though your body will die because of sin, the Spirit gives you life because you have been made right with God. The Spirit of God, who raised Jesus from the dead, lives in you. And just as God raised Christ Jesus from the dead, he will give life to your mortal bodies by this same Spirit living within you. Therefore, dear brothers and sisters, you have no obligation to do what your sinful nature urges you to do. For if you live by its dictates, you will die. But if through the power of the Spirit you put to death the deeds of your sinful nature, you will live. For all who are led by the Spirit of God are children of God." *(Romans 8:9-14 NLT)*

God is fully willing to, and capable of, fulfilling His promises to us, but we must become people who are capable of properly managing the fulfillment of those promises. Dr. Myles Munroe said "Where there is no management, God retards growth." So if you're wondering why it never seems like you're progressing toward a blessing, check to see what you've done with the current blessing. True teaching and preaching should emphasize this.

When a church is void of true teaching and preaching, training and instruction, what is the alternative? What are people getting in church if they are not getting the word and how to apply it and live it? People are still attending every Sunday, but what do they get when they go? Well, it's quite simple. They get a fix. Like any addict seeking a high, it is understand that the drug only provides a temporary escape. When the effects of the drugs wear off, their problems and issues are there waiting on them. In the absence of information and true inspiration to deal with those problems, people run from them and to the thing that provided the temporary escape.

This is what church has become to a lot of people. Pastors in these churches are dealing and pushing temporary escapes through an over-emotional display of half-truths wrapped in entertainment. Even a sermon can appeal more to the flesh than to a person's spirit and mind when it doesn't contain the principles of God that are essential for true sustenance. These pastors serve more as drug dealers than shepherds. The focus is more on keeping loyal customers than tending to the spiritual welfare of people.

Now, is this the case for all churches and pastors? Of course not! There are scores of pastors that are very devoted to and concerned about people and the state of their souls. But even one pastor who would rather fill his church by neglecting to give people the complete word of God is too many. The Lord said He desires that none would perish, but that all would come to repentance. The cost of souls is too high. Just ask Jesus, the one who paid it all.

CHAPTER 2

THE "HOOK-UP

I REMEMBER LISTENING TO STEVE HARVEY tell a joke once about Judgement Day. He talked about how there would be people standing in a long line waiting to get into Heaven. People who knew someone important in Heaven would be at the pearly gates name-dropping once they realized they didn't have enough juice to get in, like people trying to get into this exclusive place with a guest list. They would get to the gates and realize their name was not written in the Lamb's Book of Life, so that meant they were turned away and had to go to hell. As they would be walking away, they would see Jesus and call his name as if to get His attention, "Jesus...hey Jesus...Jesuuuuus!', and He would ignore them to which they would reply, "That's messed up, Jesus! It's like that? Okay then!"

Do you know someone like that? Every time you see them they're trying to get the hook-up on something! Now, it wouldn't be so bad if they were worldly, but these are Christians! There seems to be some unwritten rule that because we're both children of

God, you're supposed to benefit from your brother or sister's hard work while neglecting to do your own hard work. Christianity has become, to a lot of people, this exclusive club where the benefits are you having access to things others have all because it belongs to God. The worst part is when they try to throw a guilt trip on you for not helping them the way they feel you should have helped them. THE AUDACITY!!

Let's look at a few examples of unacceptable hook-ups that really violate a true Godly relationship, but have become pretty much expected in Christianity.

1. Using someone's employee discount to purchase things for yourself. You have no business exploiting people for their discounts, or if you're the employee, allowing people to use your discount! If the rules don't state that this is acceptable, do not do this. It may seem cool or "a blessing" to benefit from someone else's employment, but understand THIS IS NOT A BLESSING! In fact, THIS IS STEALING, an offense covered by the very basic rules of Christianity, "Thou shall not steal."

2. Getting free food or extra food when you visit another Christian employed by a restaurant or fast food establishment! This too is STEALING! This also should not be confused with a blessing. If you are the employee and you know someone who has a real need and are hungry, the proper thing to do would be to ask your employer or manager if it would be okay to do so. The ideal thing would be to just purchase the food for them with your own money. You have a job! That is your blessing. Even better than that would be for you to own the establishment yourself, and then you could hire that

person so they would have their own money to by their own food.

And if you're the person trying to get the free food from a brother or sister in Christ, it is evil of you to put them in the position to do something that would violate God's laws. I understand things get hard sometimes and you need help, but God will not set you up to do dishonest things to get what you need. Honestly, it's probably a symptom of you having too much pride to do the right thing. Humble yourself, gain employment, and do things the true "Christian" way.

3. Claiming other people's children on your taxes. This is not only a violation of God's laws, but also the laws of this nation. Pardon my slang, but YOU AIN'T GOT NO BUSINESS DOING THIS! Listen, I get it. I know times get tight and everybody else is doing it. It seems as though they manage just fine, but you are cursing yourself and tying God's hands from truly blessing you. God cannot endorse your bad behavior and improper practices. Yes, mama and your aunties and your cousins may have done it, but it is wrong. I don't care how much money they promise you if you do it, refuse. Beware of the guilt trip of "We supposed to be family!" or the classic, "That's alright! You're gonna need something one day!" Blood is thicker than water does not apply in the Kingdom of God.

4. "I want to work for a Christian business or employer!" This is the sentiment of most people with the hook-up mentality. When someone says this, typically what they mean is they want to work for someone who is not going to hold them accountable for their lack of performance on the job. They want to show up late and get off early. They want to not be fired for poor performance, and sometimes have the audacity

to expect more payment or even promotion purely on the basis that they share the same faith as their employer.

1 Timothy 5:17 says, "Let the elders that rule well be counted of double honor...", which means that your Christian employer who is serving as your elder should receive double honor from you as an employee and as a brother or sister in Christ. This means that you should work even harder to ensure their success because their success means God's success. If you're interested in God's success in the earth, you look for every opportunity to make Him look good. By being a lazy employee, who feels entitled to preferential treatment because you claim to be God's child, you not only make yourself look bad, but you discredit the name of the Lord.

These are just a few example, and sadly enough there are more out there. The Bible says to not be conformed to the patterns of this world (kosmos, governing systems on earth), but be transformed by the renewing of your mind. In other words, don't do things just because you see other people around you doing them, especially when you realize that it's wrong, no matter how popular or common it may be. Previously, you weren't as aware that these things were actually wrong, but now that the Holy Spirit has taken up residence in your heart you have more conviction that they are wrong. The problem is that culture is stronger than law. We do what we see others doing more than we do what we know is right. "Hook-ups" like these are culturally acceptable, but they go against what God says is right. They may have been your common practices before you made Christ your Lord, but that's not the case anymore. Because you have made Him your Lord you have to obey Him rather than your culture. It may take a while to break yourself from these old ways, but it is imperative that we do so.

What harm is it really? Who are you really hurting? Well, first of all, you're giving God a bad name. You've already told people that you're a Christian. They see you with your Bible on your break and hear you conveniently quoting scriptures when it suits your own agenda, so now they are watching. The issue now becomes the fact that you're supposed to be representing, or "re-presenting", Christ to those around you. In one selfish, careless act we can corrupt our witness and cause someone to look at Christ unfavorably. When you practice behavior that gives Him a bad name, He has to put a whipping on you and make an example out of you. The Apostle Paul dealt with this in his letter to the Romans.

"But if our wrongdoing only underlines and confirms God's rightdoing, shouldn't we be commended for helping out? Since our bad words don't even make a dent in his good words, isn't it wrong of God to back us to the wall and hold us to our word? These questions come up. The answer to such questions is no, a most emphatic No! How else would things ever get straightened out if God didn't do the straightening? First, there's the matter of being put in charge of writing down and caring for God's revelation, these Holy Scriptures. So, what if, in the course of doing that, some of those Jews abandoned their post? God didn't abandon them. Do you think their faithlessness cancels out his

faithfulness? Not on your life! Depend on it: God keeps his word even when the whole world is lying through its teeth. Scripture says the same: Your words stand fast and true; Rejection doesn't faze you.

It's simply perverse to say, "If my lies serve to show off God's truth all the more gloriously, why blame me? I'm doing God a favor." Some people are actually trying to put such words in our mouths, claiming that we go around saying, "The more evil we do, the more good God does, so let's just do it!" That's pure slander, as I'm sure you'll agree." (Romans 3:5-8 MSG)

He has to let people know not to follow your example. This is a huge no no!

The Word of God says that it's more blessed to give than to receive. This truth reflects a mindset of giving. This is in direct contrast to the hook-up mentality. True children of God look for opportunities to give rather than receive. If you're blessed to give, that means you have. You don't suffer from lack. I would rather be in a position to hand out blessings than standing around waiting on a handout. Now, I'm not saying that it's wrong to accept things that are given to you or even to look to people for help, but when you neglect to put forth your own effort to secure your basic needs and anticipate or even expect others to do so for you, that is not being blessed. That's mooching! And if you use your relationship as a brother or sister in Christ to guilt people in to giving to you, you are committing spiritual extortion. We should never use the fact that someone is a believer to force them to do what we want them to do, especially when God may be telling them to do just the opposite.

Now, you must understand that we will always rely on Christ for guidance, strength, protection, and even opportunities, but there comes a time where you grow from a mindset of what God can do for me (usually characterized by miracles God does on our behalf) to "Lord, what is it that you've given me the power to do for myself." This stage is generally characterized by independence. This is when you get to a place where you don't pray for God to pay your bills anymore because you've become responsible enough to secure employment that affords you the ability to pay your own bills. This is the place where we have to be extremely careful. In this place, people tend to get lost and stop relying on Christ. This is the place where people begin to neglect their walk with Christ. Why is this you say? Because up to this point God was only someone who could provide you with the things you could not provide yourself with. When you were in the dependent stage you prayed constantly for God to pay your bills, feed you, and put clothes on your back. You spent so much time doing this that eventually that's all God became to you; someone who can pay your bills. So when you moved into a place of independence, you didn't see a need for Him, other than keeping you out of sin. This is the deception that Adam and Eve fell for in the garden. The temptation wasn't being like God. We already know that they were like God because He created us in His image. The deception was that they would be like God *without needing God*.

When we reach the independence stage, we have to be careful and not get beside ourselves just because it appears now we can secure our basic needs on our own. We have to look deeper into God and see what the next level is. We get tempted to stay at this level, and most modern teachings, like the prosperity gospel, support this level as the ultimate goal. This is where you get the house, the car, and the nice clothes. In this stage you can reach back and help someone in the dependent stage. You have a few more resources, so you can pay a bill for someone or buy them something to eat. The problem is that it now becomes all about you. We can become very selfish in this stage and forget where we came from, so God has to allow things to happen to get us back to that dependent stage where we prayed, read our word, and sought after Him. Sadly, this is not the progression God is looking for in us, and we get caught in this ugly cycle of back and forth between the dependent and independent stages. As a result, we miss the ultimate stage, the interdependent stage. You never outgrow God, but rather grow in your dependence of Him. Likewise, plants never outgrow the soil. They grow in it and use the nutrients it provides in order to grow, mature, and become fruitful.

Jesus addressed this in the parable of the unfruitful fig tree (Luke 13:6-9). The master of the vineyard wanted fruit from the tree, but it wasn't producing. Its roots were in the ground, so it was benefiting from the good nutrients provided by the soil much like God provided you with the job in order for you to reach a level of independence. You got paid and neglected the fact that it's not about you, but you stay planted and grew. Your leaves become full and your branches become strong because you reach a point of maturity where it looks like you're flourishing. God looks at you and says that you look healthy and strong, and you show signs that there should be fruit, but you have yet to produce any. A tree that only has good leaves is selfish. Leaves are a way for the tree to feed itself because the leaves produce food, but God is looking for fruit. Fruit is for others to benefit. No tree eats its own fruit. So there's another level God desires from us. However, if we neglect it, He may have to uproot us, and I don't know any tree that can survive without the soil.

Here is the progression. We move from a place of "God, I need you to do for me" (dependent stage) to a place of "God, grant me the strength and wisdom to do for myself" (independent stage). But it doesn't end there. Then we have to move from "God allow me to do for myself" to 'God, I want to be a blessing and do for others" (interdependent stage). In the interdependent stage, you become fruitful and produce things that will benefit and bless those around you. You become concerned with what God is concerned with rather than your own concerns. You've mastered the principles of God in the independent stage and secured a firm place from which you can launch out on your mission for God. The interdependent stage is where we partner with God and look for ways to become an active participant in His will being accomplished in the earth. The body of Christ is an interdependent reality, and we must all ultimately strive to do our part.

□

Let me be perfectly clear. You strive to serve people in every stage, but ultimately you want to grow in your level of service. For example, let's say you like to cook, and whenever you cook you make a little extra for a few neighbors who you know don't have enough to feed themselves. You may be currently on government assistance and suffer from lack, but whenever you get your hands on enough money to cook like you want to, you always think about the people around you that you know are starving. This is a dependent stage. Next, you say you wish you could do more, so God provides you with a job and you have an opportunity not only to learn how to cook, but eventually you learn how to run a complete operation for serving large groups of people. You're working and paying your bills, but you are also growing and learning valuable skills that will allow you to effectively feed large groups of people on a larger scale. This is independence. Then you take that desire to feed people and come up with a plan for how you're going to do it. You develop the plan and work it to the point where you can open your own soup kitchen that feeds thousands of people. The soup kitchen is the fruit that God uses to bless those people, and you not only feed them, but you become a conduit through which God can reach people on a much grander scale.

So, hopefully you now understand why the "hook-up" mentality has no place in the Kingdom of God or the Body of Christ. There is too much work to be done and too many people to reach. Mentalities like that hinder us from receiving the true blessings of God and ultimately from becoming the blessing to others that God intended for us to be. It keeps us from being responsible children of the King and fruitful producers.

> *"This is the true joy in life, that being used for a purpose recognized by yourself as a mighty one. That being a force of nature instead of a feverish, selfish little clod of ailments and grievances, complaining that the world will not devote itself to making you happy. I am of the opinion that my life belongs to the whole community, and as long as I live, it is my privilege to do for it whatever I can. I want to be thoroughly used up when I die. For the harder I work, the more I live. I rejoice in life for its own sake. Life is no brief candle to me. It's a sort of splendid torch which I've got to hold up for the moment, and I want to make it burn as brightly as possible, before handing it on to future generations." - George Bernard Shaw*

CHAPTER 3

RACE TO THE PULPIT

COMING FROM A SMALL CITY, I'm very acquainted with church. Growing up, it was what you had to do; either you were in church or you were not. There was really no in-between. If your parents went to church, you went to church every time they went. This made church very popular in our city, so if anyone wanted to be great, or seem to be, all they had to do was make a name for themselves in church.

I remember the great reverence that was shown to pastors. If the pastor came over for dinner, it was likely he would get served first, and he didn't have to fix his plate! He just sat at the table and was served while everyone else had to fix their own plate. And if that wasn't enough, they usually ate out of the good China while others had to use the paper plates and cups. Plus, he got the big piece of chicken! The women in church would fall out all over him, single and married, and being that females dominated the congregation, he would have his pick. And don't be a young, single guy with any measure of good looks! You would be a virtual rock star!

In my community, the pastor was the local celebrity. He typically drove a pretty nice car and people would just give him things. He also had a lot of privileges, was well respected, and usually had nice things as it pertains to clothes, shoes, and jewelry. All this, and all you had to do was be able to get people riled up during a sermon by using clever phrases in that typical preacher tone and developing a passionate whoop. On top of that, if you could sing, OMG, you were a god! The other men wanted to be you, the women wanted to be with you, the young girls crushed on you, and the boys imitated you. The pastor had unspeakable influence!

This led to a lot of young men that had the "call" to try to make their way to the pulpit. Once you made it to the pulpit, if you had a good whoop, you were ready. You immediately made a name for yourself and the next step was to get you a church! As I sit here writing this, it's becoming more apparent to me how crazy this sounds, but pretty much that's how it went.

I visited my hometown one weekend and stopped into one of the churches I went to as a kid. It was good seeing all the people, and naturally when you see people you haven't seen in a while, they ask what you are doing now. For those that had heard that I am a minister, the question I would often get was did I have a church, as in my own church? Just the notion that because I am a minister, I must have a church reveals the thinking of some people as it pertains to ministry or the definition of a minister.

☐

What is it about modern Christianity, or the church culture, that makes us want to rush individuals to the pulpit? Does it not register with us how heavy of a responsibility that is? Obviously not because we do it all the time, especially with celebrities. Let a famous athlete or rapper merely announce that they have accepted Christ and we won't hesitate to put them up in someone's pulpit to preach! We don't even wait to hear if they believe that God has called them to serve Him in this capacity. As soon as they announce their salvation, we see them on TBN, Daystar, and all the major Christian networks where they are being broadcasted to millions of God's people. Now, I'm not saying they shouldn't give their testimony, but those allowing them access to their congregation should use caution. As a shepherd, you must protect your flock.

There are two major problems with operating this way. The first is we have to consider the effect it has on the people who are listening to the preacher. Standing before God's people and delivering a message from Him is a highly influential position, and when not properly respected, it can cause serious damage to those listening. Because of the pedestal we put preachers on in today's church, we should exercise a lot more caution when it comes to who we let stand in front of people to give a word. We have to take the time to see where these people are in their walk with Christ, before we give them access to our pulpit because their character is going to speak a lot louder than the word they delivered that Sunday morning or Wednesday night. This goes double for celebrities. They already have a significant measure of influence and if their character hasn't been proven, any flaws in that character are amplified and viewed by weaker Christians as acceptable.

The word of God is not just some good points to expound on. We often refer to it as a sword, or in modern terms maybe a gun. Nevertheless, it is recognized as a weapon. Ask yourself this, how comfortable would you feel with giving a sword or a gun to a baby? I pray you wouldn't be comfortable with it at all (you never know with the judgement displayed by some people these days). A weapon in the hands of someone who doesn't understand the power of it can be very dangerous. When we accept Christ, we are new born babes in the Kingdom, so typically we lack the maturity to properly handle the word of God as it pertains to leading people, because make no mistake, anyone who stands in front of people to deliver a word is positioned for leadership. They may not be in a leadership position per say as in holding a formal title, but they are put in a position of leadership. I've seen what happens when this is taken lightly, and it is deplorable.

A great example of this was displayed during the events surrounding the Michael Brown incident in 2014 in Missouri. Michael Brown, a young African-American teenager, was killed by a police officer. He was unarmed at the time of the shooting so the officer was put on trial. When it was time for the verdict to be handed down, the air in that neighborhood was highly volatile, and all eyes were on Michael Brown's mother. She could be the spark to ignite an uncontrollable fire or the voice of change to provoke people to a more positive course of action. When the officer was found not guilty, the cameras were rolling, and she had an honest, emotional moment that displayed her disappointment with the verdict, a moment that I personally believe she shouldn't have had in public. Because of the raw emotion of anger displayed, she struck a match which lit the fuse that resulted in an explosion of emotion that lead people to destroy their own neighborhoods in answer to that verdict. It was clear that nobody took the time to prepare her for the position of leadership she was thrusted into by the events surrounding her son and the not guilty verdict of the officer that shot him.

It takes time, preparation, and training to be ready to stand before God's people on a continuous basis. First you have to submit to the Word of God wholeheartedly. You can present the authority of His word if it is not your authority first. We no longer live in a do as I say and not as I do society. People actually look at the Bible these days, if only occasionally. Any inconsistency can be seriously damaging to people. If you honestly desire to stand and deliver God's word to His people, you have to actually care about the people enough to internalize His word yourself.

Also, you have to be properly mentored by someone who has displayed true Godly character and wisdom in handling God's word and caring for His people. You have to submit to an earthly authority. Someone has to be able to tell you when you're wrong and when you're right. You need a resource from which you can draw from their experiences. A willingness to listen to and heed their counsel is a plus as well. You should never be a lone wolf.

Wolves don't mix well with sheep. They have a tendency to want to feed on them rather than feed them.

Nobody is ready for such an awesome responsibility overnight. God has to have time to prove you. He has to take you through tests and trials to fix your character. The problem is that a lot of preachers don't have the patience required to properly develop the capacity to handle this responsibility without posing a threat to God's people. You get saved on Monday, announce your calling on Wednesday, and you're up in someone's pulpit on Sunday. Now, I'm not being literal, but just trying to make a point of how this process gets rushed. I know you say there isn't any possible way an individual would allow someone so unprepared in their pulpit, but you would be surprised. It takes time to become skilled with such a powerful weapon.

Now, the second problem with rushing to the pulpit, or allowing some to take that platform too early, is that it can seriously damage the preacher. When you rush to take on such a heavy responsibility, it's all about you and the name you're trying to make for yourself. It's more about how you look to people rather than who you are truly helping. This is not a position you want to put yourself in, because when you do you open the door for Satan to get his hooks in you. The Bible says that Jesus made himself of no reputation. Why would he go out of His way to purposefully not make a name for himself? It's because He knew that holding so tight to a reputation would limit his reach. He wanted to remain flexible so he could reach more people. Jesus ministered to people that others in society, and especially in the church (temple), thought he shouldn't associate with. He didn't have time to be concerned about who would talk about Him for ministering to a prostitute or an alcoholic. If He had allowed Himself to be consumed with the opinions of the Pharisees and Sadducees (the religious community leaders), He would have never reached out to those in desperate need of Him, and He would have been of no use to the Father. Dr. Myles Munroe used to say, "If you need the people, you can't lead the people." If you need the people, you put yourself in a position to compromise the very character that God needs you to have.

It is imperative to grow past the point where people's opinions of you matter that much and the only one you aim to please is the Lord. Being inflexible doesn't allow you to admit faults. It forces you to lie to save face with people you believe you have a good reputation with. It forces you to hide your true self and lead a double-life. It compels you to do things for the show and not for the purpose of serving the Lord, all because you have to keep that reputation intact. Nobody can ever tell you anything because you have to act like you know it already. You have to maintain this air of superiority and you can never humble yourself to the point of taking criticism or correction. It also causes you to be threatened when someone with a comparable or slightly better reputation comes around. You love the privilege of position, so whenever that is threatened, you naturally resort to self-preservation, which leads you to lie, cheat, steal, and in some instances, even kill. (I hope by now you're getting the point).

This is actually a sign of a weak character fueled by insecurities, the same insecurities that lead you to seek out this reputation as a preacher in the first place. These insecurities come from you not knowing who you are in Christ to begin with. This is what you need to find out instead of making a run for the pulpit. Honestly, that's what the "call" is all about. God is calling you to get with Him and find your true purpose. He knows that once you figure out that He intentionally created you for a specific reason because of something He wanted done in the earth, then maybe you would partner with Him in the process of changing you rather than fighting Him. You desire greatness, and God is telling you He created you to be great but in the way He purposed you to be. If you're going to achieve this type of greatness, patience must be applied.

It takes time to form a Godly character, but you have to understand why it is so important in the life of anyone who wants to lead people. We know that God is unchanging. He's the same yesterday, today, and forever. That unchanging quality of God is His character. It's this quality that allows us to depend on Him. It's the essence of His holiness. God says, "...and ye shall be holy, for I am holy..." (Leviticus 11:44, KJV). If you notice, letters of the alphabet are called characters. The letter "B" will always be the letter B, and we depend on it remaining as such because it brings stability to whatever we read. If "B" was always changing and shifting, it would make words unsure and hard to read. As a pastor, preacher, or leader in that capacity, your character has to be fixed because there are people depending on you being who you are all the time. They're basing aspects of their lives on this fact. When you're shifty, it makes those aspects of their life unsure, which breeds insecurity and uncertainty. Those things make people desperate, and desperate people do things that God doesn't agree with.

This is what it means when we call Christ the "rock" of our salvation. He's solid and dependable. We can build our entire lives on the fact of who He is. I have a friend who is a structural engineer, and he can attest to the fact that when you're constructing a building, you look for a rock in the earth on which to lay your foundation. It assures that your building will be solid and will stand the test of time. The same goes for ministries, families, businesses, and any other things you plan on building that affects people's lives. You have to be solid and dependable. It takes time for God to get you there, but make no mistake about it, this is what God wants more than anything for you. It's called being "conformed" into the image of Christ (Romans 8:29). Christ's character has been proven as dependable. Ours hasn't. God has to get us to be a character that He can trust. That character is Christ. In 1 Corinthians 11:1, the Apostle Paul says, "Follow my example, as I follow the example of Christ. (NIV)" If you haven't fully settled in on the idea of following Him, don't jump at the chance to be put in a position for others to follow you.

Be careful when running for the spotlight. Light has a way of exposing things. If you have things that you don't want exposed, it may be best to avoid the spotlight for awhile. Look to serve people first, and find out what the "call" of God on your life is all about. Allow Him the time to construct your character, and let Him put you in that light. This way you're protected from a fall, your family is protected from the shame, and the people who make the decision to follow you are protected from you.

CHAPTER 4

FINDING YOUR PULPIT

IN THE LAST CHAPTER, we talked about the eagerness some young ministers show when it comes to getting to the pulpit. In the church there's only one pulpit, and if you have a lot of ministers it could bring about a lot of competition, which may not be the best thing. There's nothing wrong with wanting to be the best. The late Ernest Hemingway said, "There's no nobility in being superior to your fellow man. True nobility is being superior to your former self." But in a church atmosphere competition can foster a lot of negative emotions and behavior. Competition can bring out the ugly side of some of the holiest of Christians. If you don't believe me, go and watch some of these church league basketball games.

Even Jesus' disciples dealt with this competitive issue. In the twentieth chapter of Matthew (verses 20 through 27), the mother of two of the disciples, James and John, approached Jesus asking for the top positions for her sons when He came into his kingdom (most assumed that He was going to establish an earthly kingdom during that time, restoring Israel to its former glory). Naturally, mothers want the best for their children, so she was trying to help out (her sons didn't seem to mind), but the other disciples were watching all of this and they were not happy about it. After Jesus settled the issue with the mother, He noticed the murmuring of the other ten and called them all to Him. Now, the interesting thing is He didn't rebuke them for their desire to be great, but rather told them how to actually become great. He said that the one who desires to be greatest must become the minister (servant) of all.

Oftentimes, because of our Christian paradigm, we assume that "servant" means waiting on people hand and foot, like a butler or slave, but that's not what is meant here. This form of servitude means to provide a service. You are a servant of God, but you provide a service to His people and the world around you. People that work for the government are called civil "servants". That doesn't mean that you can boss them around and they have to take orders from you, but rather they are fulfilling some type of necessary duty on behalf of the government to assist the citizens.

The term used in the King James Version of Matthew 20:26 is "minister". This word or term has been greatly abused by today's church. Minister has become just a title that supposedly affords you some privilege and respect in church, and also licenses you for the opportunity to stand behind someone's pulpit. Some people will go as far as correct people when they don't address them a Minister So-and-so! REALLY?! This type of behavior truly gets under my skin personally. This is not the true meaning of minister or ministry. The truth of the matter is that if most people knew the true meaning of ministry or minister, they wouldn't sign up for it so quickly.

The term seems to be lost to us here in the United States. This is largely due to the separation of church and state. In foreign countries, the governmental services are called "ministries". You have a Ministry of Finance that handles the finances of the government. There's also a Ministry of Defense that oversees the countries defenses, and a Ministry of Justice that oversees areas of constitutional policies. Even the head official of the government is called the Prime Minister! So if you go to certain countries and state that you're a minister, they want to know what service you are providing. But in the U.S., if you tell someone you're a minister, their first question is what church do you go to. They want to know how long you've been preaching, rather than asking how long you've been serving. Service capacity is the furthest thing from their mind!

In Christianity today, the term, or title, seems to have more of a negative effect on those who say they are "called". Our limited perspective, and abuse, of ministry almost neutralizes people. It relegates them to only serving in a church building and preaching. If they do any work outside of the church, it's typically only handling the interests of a certain congregational body. A probably more disappointing fact is that sometimes you can have a church full of ministers and still can't accomplish anything. You have to constantly look for people to actually serve in the various areas of the church that need people helping out. The pastor has to stand up and practically beg people to lend a hand to get things done. Oh but let him say he needs somebody to preach!! You would have to beat them away from that pulpit with a stick! I mean, is it just me or does anyone else see something terribly wrong with this scenario?

For arguments sake, let's say you have a person, who we'll call John, working in the banking industry. He has one of the greatest financial minds of our time and his career has been stellar. He's received various types of recognitions, accolades, and has been promoted several times in just a few years. As he moves up the corporate ladder, he notices some practices in banking that he's not comfortable with. Maybe he saw innocent people being taken advantage of or a common practice of poor business ethics that begins to give him a negative view of the industry he's seemed to excel in. He loved his work once, but now has began to lose interest because he doesn't see things getting better in the industry. Then one day John announces that he has been "called". Because of the Christian perspective of ministry, he feels compelled to leave the banking industry where he's showed so much promise and go into full-time ministry. He goes to Bible school, gets ordained, and becomes a full-time minister at the church where he preaches occasionally, teaches Sunday school, leads a men's group, and even oversees a particular ministry in the church. The only time he uses that great financial mind is when he helps count the offering after each service. The church has now successfully neutralized a person with a God-given ability to operate in the world of banking and finance.

What if the calling that John felt at that time was really a burden to see the unethical practices in the banking industry change? What if the call of God he felt was Christ actually saying to him, "John, you see all this mess going on in this industry? I want it changed. I don't want my people being abused and taken advantage of financially. I want the knowledge of Me and My ways to now be in the decision-making arenas of the banking industry and I'm calling on you to make this happen for Me." What if rather than oversee a ministry in a church, John was called to oversee the whole banking system for one of the major banks in his city? That can't effectively happen with John no longer being a part of that industry. In the words of the late Dr. Munroe, "You can never change what you avoid."

John's story is a common occurrence in Christianity today. I've heard of, and witnessed myself, many different accounts of people who left their profession to pursue the call of ministry on their lives. The call takes them out of the true place that God has called them to and immediately puts them on the path to the pulpit. Now, with our current paradigm, this quest for the pulpit is a problem, but I would like to offer you a different perspective. One that may empower the Johns of this life rather than neutralize them.

If you have ever been inside a church before, I'm sure you're familiar with the physical pulpit. It's typically an elevated platform with a podium of some sort. Typically, the pastor or preacher stands behind it when preaching a sermon. It's considered by many to be a sacred spot, so much so that some people thought that God would strike you down if you played around or walked behind it. I've never seen Him strike anyone down for it, but those church mothers posed a serious threat. That pulpit is obvious, but I heard my pastor give his definition of a pulpit once, and to make my point, I would like to use what he said as the working definition of the word. He said a pulpit is the place from which you stand and pull people from the pits of hell. I love this definition! It doesn't limit the pulpit to just a sacred spot behind a podium in a church. The possibilities with this definition could potentially lead us to many different, new, and exciting areas of ministry. Let's examine it further.

Typically, when we witness to unsaved people, we speak to them about salvation from the eternal hell that awaits unbelievers after the final judgement. The problem is that many of them can't wrap their mind around a pit of hell where they will burn for eternity because they can't see past the pit of hell they're currently enduring. They're living in pits of despair, hopelessness, debt, broken homes, broken marriages, generational curses, drug and sex addictions, and a host of others. There was a time in this country where the church represented a place of hope to the world around it, but those days have all but gone. No longer are the people coming to church who are currently enduring their own pit. They're not experiencing that word of hope and salvation from the pulpit located there. How do we reconnect them with the pulpit so they can be pulled from their current pit of hell? Wouldn't it be nice if we could take the pulpit out of the church and put it in the places where life is happening?

Great news!! We can!! Consider this. In the church, the pulpit is a place of influence. It's a spot where, if you are the preacher, you are elevated. The attention is drawn to you and everyone hangs onto the words you speak from that place. So we just need to find a place outside of the church where you have influence; a preverbal spot where you're elevated and the attention is drawn to you. I present to you that this place is your gift. It's the thing that God has given you that promotes your influence and position. It's the light that God endowed you with that draws everyone's attention to you, and once you have their attention, you declare the goodness of God to the world.

I know what you're thinking, "But, I'm not a preacher or pastor!" This is one of the biggest problems with Christianity today. When we hear the word "preach", we immediately reserve that job for ministers in church. Our limited thinking is limiting our reach. The Bible says, "How, then, can they call on the one they have not believed in? And how can they hear without someone preaching to them? And how can they preach unless they are sent?" (Romans 10:14-15a, NIV). Preaching is for anyone with a desire for people to believe in God. If you believe that God is THE answer and people should believe in Him, then you should preach. Our current way of thinking pushes us to try to get people to the church so our pastor

□

can preach to them and they can hear the word of God, but the scripture clearly says we must be sent. It didn't say that we must persuade them to come to church with us. So the first thing we have to do is take Christ out of that box called the four walls of the church and look for new creative ways to take the word of God to people outside the church.

Now, the truth of the matter is not everyone can stand up in church behind a pulpit and preach a sermon. I know people who break out into cold sweats when they have to stand in front of anyone and speak, let alone deliver a message from God, but we can develop our gift and God-given purpose to attract the attention of the world. Truthfully, some people don't care too much for the word of God because they've seen it abused so much, but it's hard for the world to ignore excellence. Once you cultivate your gift to the point that you are operating in and displaying excellence, people will notice you. If Lebron James wasn't one of the best basketball players in the world, how many of us would even know of him? However, it's because of the God-given gift he has to play the game, and the hard work he's put in to cultivate that gift, that causes us to take notice of him. Basketball is Lebron James' pulpit. It's the place where he has influence. It's the spot where he's elevated and the attention of the world is drawn to him. What would happen if during an interview, maybe like the one he had when he announced his move to the Miami Heat, Lebron stated that the key contributing factor to his success was the time he spends with God before he practices and plays? What if during that same interview, he said he never leaves home without his Bible? I tell you that, although the Bible is the best-selling book ever, the Christian stores wouldn't be able to keep them on the shelves! You would start seeing Bibles in the athletic stores on the next isle over from the basketball shoes!

Listen, your gift is your pulpit and your sermon is your faithful service to God and obedience to His word. What do you do when you admire someone's gift and their ability to display that gift at such a level that they stand apart from others? Often, we look deeper into their lives to see what makes them who they are. People will often become a fan. Fans seems to know a lot about the people they admire. They know their favorite food, their birthdates, their work regimen, their health and beauty secrets, and countless other things. Further than that, many fans will adopt the practices of that celebrity into their own lives. That's the power of endorsements. Advertisers know that once a person has a recognizable name, they have influence over people and once that person mentions they use their product, many of the people who are familiar with that celebrity will go out and get that product. God is looking for people who have developed their gift and are operating in their purpose to endorse His word.

What are you developing in your life to draw people? What is it you do better than anyone else that causes you to stand out? God has given everyone a gift. He's given us all a pulpit, something that elevates us and catches the attention of those around us. Maybe you have this incredible speaking voice where everyone seeks you out to do voiceovers or television and radio announcements. Maybe you have a love for biology and two of the most steady hands in the world that allow you to become a world-renowned surgeon. Perhaps you have incredible speed and the ability to break world records. Whatever it is that God has given you, He gave it to you with the intent of you making His name great. People seek you out, but it's not for you to elevate yourself. God elevates you. The Bible says that nobody lights a candle and hides it, but rather they place it upon a stand so that it can give light to the whole house. That light speaks of your influence. It's the specific light He's given you, but it is your responsibility to shine. God, in turn, provides you with the opportunity to display that light to the world. Your responsibility is to bring Him glory by using that attention people give you as an opportunity to show them the hope, joy, and fulfillment that is in Christ Jesus. It's this hope that causes people to find out who He is and discover their hope in Him as well. You can be the vessel Christ uses to pull someone from the pits of abuse, low self-esteem, generational curses, and poverty. At the end of the day, all that matters are the people we win to Christ. We believe that He is the answer to all that ails this world because we know what He did for us. It is that truth that pushes us to cultivate our gifts in preparation for that nuclear moment where time, opportunity, and preparation all come together. In that moment, the undeniable truth of Christ becomes clear to all people. You see, God doesn't just want us to bless others. He wants us to be a blessing to others. He wants our entire life to be a book that people read and discover the wonders of

His grace, mercy, and love. In the words of Leo Rosten, "The purpose of life is not to be happy — but to matter, to be productive, to be useful, to have it make some difference that you have lived at all." You matter to God, so find your pulpit and show God that His people matter to you.

CHAPTER 5

WHAT IS "CHURCH SERVICE"?

"First they ignore you, then they ridicule you, then they fight you, and then you win." - Mahatma Gandhi

IN JOHN 15:18, Jesus states that, "If the world hates you, know that it hated Me before it hated you." (Amplified). In this passage, Jesus was not only talking to His disciples, but also to the church (body of Christ) as a whole. This hatred, or opposition to Christ and His ways, the world has towards the church is natural friction. Day after day, we encounter a world that does not subscribe to the same beliefs and ways that we who belong to Christ do. These encounters wear on us during the week. On our jobs, in the malls, the schools, at the supermarket, and even sometimes in our own homes. We have to stand against the ways of the world. For example, your boss asks you to do something unethical, but you refuse because it goes against what Christ says is right. You may have unbelieving friends that don't particularly agree with your new belief system, so they constantly remind you of who you were before you gave your life to Christ in the effort to secure their own comfort in their wrongdoings. Maybe there's a young man or young lady who begins to spread false rumors about you because you won't "put out". All this friction begins to wear on you mentally, spiritually, and maybe even physically (stress), so what do you do? Where do you go to get what you need to maintain in this Christian walk?

I'm no auto mechanic, but I am an engineer and I remember studying the function of automobile engines in college. Engines have many moving parts that encounter a natural force called friction. Friction is not a negative thing. Just like any other principle in nature, it just is, like gravity for instance. You can't really avoid it, just manage its effects.

Friction creates heat, which can be good or bad for engines. If properly managed, this heat can be a plus. Engines work better at a certain operating temperature, so this heat helps the engine reach that temperature, allowing the engine to run more efficiently. In a like manner, God uses heat to help us as well. Consider 1 Peter 4:12-13 which says, "Beloved, think it not strange concerning the fiery trial which is to try you, as though some strange thing happened unto you: But rejoice, inasmuch as ye are partakers of Christ's sufferings; that, when his glory shall be revealed, ye may be glad also with exceeding joy." That same heat, however, is also the thing that begins to wear out those moving parts, and that entire engine will begin to lose power, and eventually, if not properly maintained, will shut down completely. In order to prevent the loss of power and malfunction of the engine, you must have it serviced.

Anywhere you find automobiles, you will typically find businesses established for the sole purpose of helping you maintain your vehicle. They are called service and repair centers or shops. The service aspect is for prevention whereas repair is to fix something that has stopped working properly. Probably the most common of these service centers is the oil change shop. Oil is the vital thing your engines needs to help it handle the heat from the friction. It helps those moving parts interact with each other without shutting down on one another. Automobiles are necessary in our daily lives, but they must be serviced so we can continuously benefit from their function.

What does this have to do with "church service"? Well, there are places for automobiles to get "serviced" when the heat from the friction in the engine begins to wear on the parts, so what about the church (body of Christ)? The Church also encounters friction when it is functioning. Where can we go to get that service we need? We go to our local house of worship, the place where the "church" gets "serviced"!

The current paradigm of church for many Christians today limits the church's effectiveness because it doesn't model Christ's intent for the church. Some of the common phrases you may have heard like "I'm going to church" or "We had some good church today" clue us in on how we've gotten the wrong understanding of church. Phrases like these make the church just a destination you go to a couple of days out of the week or just an experience where you get a good feeling to help you cope with life (like our drug comparison mentioned in chapter 1). This paradigm makes the church a place (destination) of inspiration (good feeling) only. Thomas Edison said, "Genius is one percent inspiration and ninety-nine percent perspiration." That causes us to leave out the majority of what's needed to experience the genius in the mind of Christ.

First, we must understand the purpose of the Church in order to really understand what church service is all about. To really grasp this understanding, we must look at the first mention of church by Jesus Christ, our King (this title is very significant to a correct understanding of church so please take note of it). Jesus was conversing with His disciples at Caesarea Philippi in the sixteenth chapter of Matthew, and He began asking them who did people say He was. Well, if you're familiar with this conversation you know that the disciple Peter, by revelation from the Father, stated that Jesus was the Christ, which means "anointed king". Jesus then said that on this rock, the revelation of Jesus' true identity, He would build His church. There are two concepts we must grasp here in order to fully understand the church. One is the meaning of the word church. Church here is actually the Greek word "ekklesia" which means "called out ones". This makes the church a group of people rather than a group event you attend. The other thing to notice is the distinction Jesus made in saying "MY" church. Why didn't He say THE church? The church, or ekklesia, was not a religious group, but rather a governmental one. Also, only a king could have an ekklesia. That's why Peter's revelation of Jesus as The Christ, or anointed King, was so significant. Only kings have ekklesias. Caesar had an ekklesia, hence the distinction Christ made in saying HIS church. The purpose of this group of "called out ones" was to record the will of the king and make it public knowledge and law in the land. You wonder why the knowledge of Christ is steadily diminishing from society? It's because we have reduced church to a good feeling and lost the concept of its original intent.

Since we now know who the church was meant to be, what is it meant to do? It's really quite simple. The church was created to work. We just mentioned that the purpose of the ekklesia was to ensure that the knowledge and will of the King were known to everyone in the land. This requires work. This has become an ugly word for most Christians today. We've made the gospel of Christ simply about existing and getting a few people saved in the process. There's a story I heard a man tell once that may illustrate today's Christian's approach to church. The gentleman said he had a nice little place in Hawaii by the water and he would sit in his office to work on his book. This was before computers, because he mentions having the pages of his book stacked on his desk. He was writing one day and decided to open a window to let in the ocean breeze that he enjoyed so much. Suddenly, the light breeze quickly turned to heavier gusts of wind and began to blow the pages of his book across the room onto the floor. He began to scurry about the room frantically gathering them, trying to regain the order of the pages, while the wind was still working against him reducing the effects of his effort. During this frustrating exercise, the most brilliant thought came to his mind..."Close the window". That is pure genius!

I'm being facetious with the genius remark, but we take the same approach to reaching people for Christ. We frantically go about life scrambling to help people know Christ and maintain some order in their lives, but we never address the wind that is blowing and working contrary to our efforts. The church today seems to always take a reactive approach of getting people to know Christ. The church was designed to shut the windows of life that blow things out of order. If we would shut more windows, it would make it easier to organize the madness and bring to light the knowledge of Christ that gets people's lives in order. This requires us to be proactive in our approach. It's the church letting people come rather than obeying the command of Christ to GO into all the world. "The world is a dangerous place to live; not because of the people who are evil, but because of the people who don't do anything about it." - Albert Einstein. Needless to say, it's vital for the church to work.

Going back to our earlier automobile reference, the purpose of a car or truck is to do work of some kind, be it transporting people from one place to another or carrying a heavy load. As we have just discussed, the purpose of the church is to work. Cars that don't work never require service; neither do churches. We have greatly misunderstood the work we are called to do. The work we do for Christ, we call it service. There are a vast amount of people that attend a local house of worship Sunday after Sunday and call it service. We do so and believe we have fulfilled our service to God. That is foolish thinking. This misconception of service is another hindrance to our effectiveness as the church. Romans 11:35 says, "Who has given to God, that God should repay Him?" Listen, we can't "service" God. The very title God means self-sufficient one, so there is nothing we can do to make Him more God than He is already. Jesus said that if we love Him, we must feed His sheep. Our service to God is towards His people, and we honestly think we fulfill this requirement by showing up on Sunday!

The work we do for Christ by serving people is an everyday job. It's this day-in, day-out working that causes us to be worn out because in the process we encounter a world that is working against God (friction). If we don't get serviced, we can overheat. Christians that overheat usually do something that's ungodly. This is where church service comes in. The body of Christ needs to be refreshed and replenished to continue the day to day work of serving Christ. Maybe that coworker you've been trying to reach keeps trying your patience, and you neglected to go get serviced the previous Sunday or Wednesday night, so you overheat and curse that person out. Usually, this happens when we're getting close to a breakthrough with the people we're trying to reach. The service that takes place in the house of God is not us rendering service to Him, but rather Him rendering service to us. It's God giving us what we need to continue to go into the world and make His knowledge, and will, known to everyone in the land.

The funny thing is we love to call God on His promises, but

we don't want to work. When we're broke, it's nothing for us to say, "Jesus, you said in your word that the wealth of the wicked is laid up for the just!", or when we're sick to say "Lord, you said in your word that by Your stripes I'm healed!" I've never seen a company give a person a salary and health benefits simply because they like them. These are given to employees because the company needs them to do WORK! How is it that we understand this when it comes to our jobs, but we think God should just render these services to us just because He loves us? The promises of God are sure, but they're not there just to enable us to sit around and do nothing. They are for us to continue the work we are doing for the family business. There's a story in the bible where the scribes and Pharisees in the temple got upset with Jesus for healing a woman in the temple on the sabbath. The reference Jesus used to justify the healing of the woman was interesting. He asked those who challenged Him which of them does not loose their ox or donkey on the sabbath from the stall and allow them to get water? He mentioned the ox and the donkey which are commonly referred to as beasts of burden. This means the purpose of these animals is to do work. It almost implies that there was work for this woman to do, and because she was a child of Abraham, or works for the family business, she's entitled to the company's health insurance policy. The purpose of salvation is to loose us from the bonds of sin so we can get to the work of carrying out God's will in the earth.

Ask yourself this, "If we look for God to do everything, why does He need us? Wouldn't that make us unnecessary? And if we're unnecessary, why not take us on to glory as soon as we get saved? I know people often say that we were created to worship God, but based on our understanding of worship, the bible never mentions any prayers that Adam had to pray or songs he sang. In fact, the first requirement of Adam was work. In Genesis 2:15, it states that God placed the man in the garden to dress it and keep it. I will admit I'm not the sharpest tool in the shed, but dress it and keep it don't seem like commands to sing and pray. Please do not misunderstand me. I'm not saying prayer is not important. The bible says that men should always pray, and there are many references to Christ praying, but if you notice, whenever Jesus finished praying, He started working. We use prayer as means to get God to work when really it's for us to find out what is the work we should be doing. Jesus also said that the Father is always working, so He must work. I don't believe the Father's work ended with Jesus. If you read His word, you will also find this to be true.

Jesus said that greater works we would do. Plain and simple, work produces. This means that as believers, we should be producing. What are we producing? We're producing fruit. We're commanded to be fruitful. There's a principle of production called the P/PC balance, as introduced by Dr. Stephen Covey. The P (production) must be balanced with the PC (production capability, or ability to produce). Anything that produces must be maintained or else it will lose that ability to produce. Even in working for God, it's important to be refreshed and replenished with necessary resources. On the flip side, it's evil to constantly use God's resources and never produce anything. The warning of this came in the form of a parable Jesus told about a tree that would produce. The owner of the vineyard required fruit, but the tree wasn't producing so he demanded the tree be destroyed. The husbandman, or person responsible for the upkeep of the tree, pleaded with the owner to let him work with on the tree to see if he could get it to produce. Unfortunately, the tree met its demise after it would not produce.

As the church, we should be producing and also making sure we maintain that ability to produce. This is why we must understand the purpose of church service. The church has to be serviced to continue the productive work we've been called by Christ to complete. Everything done in worship on Sunday morning should be to help you in your effort to work for Christ. Whether it's an answer or solution received in prayer, the inspiration through a song, the instruction through teaching of the word, or just the refocusing from being around other believers, the Sunday morning experience should lead to a week of fruitful endeavors. Be sure to get what you need whenever you come to the house of God, so God can get what He needs out of you, which is people coming into the knowledge of Christ and making the decision to give their lives to Him.

CHAPTER 6

UNITING THE BODY OF CHRIST

"The deepest level of communication is not communication, but communion. It is wordless ... beyond speech ... beyond concept."
- Thomas Merton

A FEW YEARS BACK, I REMEMBER GOING through my news feed on Facebook and coming across a question one of my Facebook friends was asking. The question came at the end of a rather emotionally charged comment about the church being judgmental hypocrites. The particular issue being addressed was the church's stance on the alternative lifestyles some people have chosen to live. The person was stating how the people in church are not perfect, but they love to judge other people for their imperfections and sins. They mentioned how the divorce rate is high among Christians, the exposure of the secret lives of certain prominent pastors, and a few other things that you can find on the World Wide Web. So in light of these issues, how could the church judge anyone in the world for the wrong they do?

As a believer, naturally, my first reaction was to defend the church's position on the topic in question. I mentally gathered my defense and prepared to type a reply that would set my friend straight once and for all, but before my fingers could stroke the keys, the Lord brought to my remembrance a scene from the movie Remember the Titans starring Denzel Washington. In this particular scene, the Titans were in the locker room during halftime of the championship game, one that would prove to be their greatest challenge. They had managed to remain undefeated the whole season, but probably more amazing than that, the team, made up of black and white athletes attending a newly desegregated school in a racially divided town, had managed to put their differences aside and come together to be a great team. Although the athletes had come together, the coaches still had not really done so, and this tremendous opponent had begun to expose the divide between the coaches. Needless to say, they were getting whipped by a great team.

Well, in this particular scene, as the worn out players sat down, Coach Boone (played by Denzel Washington) begins to concede to defeat. He tells the guys that he's proud of them and their effort, and win or lose, they did their best which is all anyone could ask of them. As Coach Boone ends his noble speech, one of the leaders on the team, Julius Campbell, stands and says these words...

"With all due respect, you demanded more of us. You demanded

perfection. Now, I ain't saying that I'm perfect, 'cause I'm not. And I ain't gonna never be. None of us are. But we have won every single game we have played till now. So this team is perfect. We stepped out on that field that way tonight, and if it's all the same to you, Coach Boone, that's how we want to leave it." (Remember The Titans, Disney Films)

This being the inspirational highlight of the movie, of course the coaches got their act together and the team went on to win the championship.

The words of Julius Campbell resonated in my heart as he said that despite the imperfections of the individuals on the team, the team itself was perfect. So it is with the body of Christ. The body of Christ is made up of individuals who are not perfect, but Jesus Christ was perfect while He walked this earth, so ideally the body of Christ is perfect. While it is unfortunate that this perfection is currently only an ideal, the reality of its possibility still remains.

Much like the coaches in the story of Remember the Titans, the body of Christ has failed to come together, at least from what we see in this country. As long as things were good, the conflict between the coaches wasn't really a factor. The same can be said for the church in America. As long as the moral compass of the United States continued to point toward the Christian values held by the founders of this nation, the division in the body of Christ was not an issue that was felt in society like it is today. Yes, there were people who felt that we should unify, but there was no real opposition to highlight the body's division or the issues that fostered it. Let's take a quick look at the prominent issues affecting the church's ability to unify.

Why Aren't We Unified?

Lack of Commitment

Following Christ has been reduced to the type of "follow" we see on social media cites where people just click "Like" on your page to keep up with whatever's new with you. The very word "commitment" is used very loosely. We see the evidence of this truth in the way people approach relationships today. Husbands and wives won't commit to their marriage. Most married couples, even Christian ones, enter marriage with a sense of divorce at least in the back of their minds. Fathers don't commit to their children. It's become too comfortable for guys to walk away from that responsibility. People don't commit to jobs anymore. A person working for one company twenty and thirty years is virtually a thing of the past. The very idea of commitment is pretty much lost in today's society.

Probably, the most tragic loss of commitment this society is experiencing is the loss of a commitment to excellence. This lack of commitment has contributed to a decline in quality across the board, even the quality of churches. Greatness requires excellence, and excellence is measured against a standard. For the church, that standard is Christ, but we don't measure ourselves against standards. Today, we measure ourselves against others. As long as we're doing just as good as or better than others around us, we're fine. This fuels mediocrity within the church. Everyone, even Christians have become too comfortable with doing just enough to get by. It's based on capacity, what you're capable of doing. Goodness is the measure against something relatable. We say we want greatness, but we never reach for the standard. It requires a level of commitment we're not willing to give.

Uniting the body of Christ requires commitment to something greater than you. It's the higher calling we should press towards. We must first commit to the life Christ has called us to live and then commit to upholding that life for ourselves and everyone else in the body. It's no good if my brother in Christ commits to excellence in his daily living and I choose to do otherwise. Because we are of the same body, my lack of commitment will reflect badly on him. I must commit for the sake of fellow believers as well. This commitment is called love, and it's required for bringing the body together.

Lack of Trust

Another factor that keeps the body of Christ from unifying is the lack of trust we have towards God and one another. It's become cultural in this nation to trust no-one. That lack of trust has spilled over into the church. Everything in our society compels us the look out for ourselves first, even at the expense of other's well-being. We are instructed by commercials to do what feels good to us first. It's become people's expectation to look for someone you trust to hurt you, so you do it to them before they do it to you. Even in the church, we fail to truly open our hearts to the type of relationship that fosters true unity.

I remember listening to a speech by author and professional management coach, Patrick Lencioni, where he talked about his book The Five Disfunctions of a Team. The first thing he mentioned was lack of trust was a major contributor to a team not functioning properly. He said there are two types of trust. Predictive trust is where we know what someone's actions or reaction will be based on knowing that person for a period of time. This is the trust we see most in the church. The second form, the type that makes a team work, is vulnerability-based trust. This is where we can trust people with our flaws and imperfections, typically without them being used as a means of control or ridicule. This type of trust is almost non-existent in the church.

We are almost forced to carry on a persona of perfection. Nobody wants people to see what's wrong with them, even though the church is supposed to be the one place where you can air your shortcomings in the hope that someone can help you overcome them. James 5:16 instructs of to confess our faults one to another, and pray one for another, so that we may be healed. Think about that, the sickness you're suffering from, be it mental or physical, could be healed by you opening us and letting the church know what's really wrong with you. (Now when I say "church", I mean those who have shown some sign that they believe in Jesus Christ, not just random people on the membership roster at your local house of worship. Sadly, they are not always one in the same.) Many of us would choose to hold on to that sickness because it could be easier to deal with than someone betraying your trust. Betrayal is one of the most negative marks on the church today. It absolutely kills unity.

Lack of Belief

You would think that belief would not be an issue in the church, but unfortunately it is. I don't believe we know what real belief is anymore, but it's one of the first requirements of salvation. Romans 10:9 tells us, "That if you confess with your mouth, 'Jesus is Lord,' and believe in your heart that God raised Him from the dead, you will be saved. (NIV)" Now, I want you to notice something key. In that verse it said that the belief must be in your heart. That word heart means subconscious mind. This is the place where our habits are stored. When someone actually believes something, you don't have to wonder. It shows without them having to purposefully let you know. For instance, a person that's afraid of dogs doesn't have to tell you they're afraid of dogs. If you want to see what they believe, just let a dog get anywhere near them. Their actions will tell you they are afraid of dogs. If we truly believe in Christ, we don't have to always go around telling people. They will automatically know by our actions.

Much of what we call belief today is just a mental acknowledgment that we like the story of Jesus. Most of us are like, "He's a cool guy who did some cool things. And on top of that, he died on a cross for me. Anyone who does that for me is okay in my book." There's a huge difference in liking Christ and committing (there's that word again) your whole life to Him and His ways. You want to be so into Christ that when He thinks, you think. When He speaks, you speak. When He shows compassion, you show compassion. It's how we represent, or re-present, Christ to the world.

The church has reduced belief to an outward appearance. We believe that once a person says the prayer of salvation, all we have to do is put them on some nice clothes, give them a fresh haircut or do, teach them the vernacular, and they are right for heaven! We never really address their heart and the issues that live their. This type of belief, or rather the lack of true belief, causes us to fail in our effort to really love people. Real love takes time and effort. In today's microwave society, most of us don't have that kind of time, so the body of Christ suffers. True belief compels us to carry out the command of love given by Christ, which causes us to have the type of patience required for unity to take place.

Lack of Community

If you look at the groups of people that truly impact America with their culture, you will see one thing they all have in common. They all have a sense of community. They have an overall sense of some mission they want to accomplish that their personal issues always take a back seat to. They don't all agree on the same things within their community, but when they address the rest of society, they have that one thing they all agree on that breeds solidarity between the members of that community. They use their oneness to get the results they desire.

I know some people will take issue with this, but let's look at the LGBTQ community. If you take a step back and look at what they've accomplished, their sense of community is undeniable. All differences and issues aside, they have quietly taken the original church's model of community and made it work for them. They agree on what they believe, they make their mission and goals clear to everyone within and without their community, and they stress excellence within their community. You may have never even noticed that they're called the LGBTQ community, at least not to where you gave real credence to the fact.

There is power when people come together. It's evident in many places in the bible. At the Tower of Babel, God said, "Behold, they are one people, and they have all one language, and this is only the beginning of what they will do; and now nothing they have imagined they can do will be impossible to them. (Amplified)" The bible also says that one can put a thousand to flight and two can put ten thousand to flight, signifying the power of unity. If the world can come together to produce works of unrighteousness, how much more can the unified body of Christ do with the power of the Holy Spirit?

Selfishness

Ralph Waldo Emerson said, "There is no limit to what can be accomplished if it doesn't matter who gets the credit." This statement rings true for anyone who has ever put it to the test. People love to get the credit for things that are accomplished. That's not the problem. The problem comes when this love clouds their vision on the work that needs to be accomplished. They would rather let the greater work suffer and go undone so they can do the smaller works and hear their names mentioned. They take on tasks that only they can complete themselves or take forever to complete them because they are doing everything themselves, and all for the sake of getting all the credit.

The minute you start talking about uniting the body of Christ, after what can be accomplished and what resources are needed is discussed, typically the next question that is asked is who's going to lead? I hate to be the person to say it, but pastors can be the worst when in comes to this. Don't get me wrong. This is not an attack on pastors, but if you want to see what I'm talking about, try getting the pastors in your city together to do some great work. There's this spirit in the church that once you get that title, humbling yourself becomes tougher. It appears that it's hard for church leaders to be vulnerable enough to show they have flaws and weaknesses to the point they admit they need other people. There are leaders who will get fighting mad if you leave their titles or credentials of their name on a program or flyer, or if you don't properly address them in public. Now, this is not all church leaders, but there are enough of them out there with this attitude to prevent the body from uniting the way it should.

This is not the model we received from Christ. He humbled himself to the point of laying aside His divinity to accomplish the greatest work ever, a work that we who have accepted Him as Lord have all benefited from. It was a completely selfless act. It was the work that motivated Him and drove Him to give His very life. We can't seem to focus on the work because we want to know who's going to get the credit for it. As a result, not only does the church suffer, but the entire world because when we fail to see past ourselves, we fail to be the sons of God. The bible testifies that the whole earth is in pain waiting for the manifestation of the sons of God.

Jesus addressed this selfishness with Peter when He washed the disciples' feet. When Peter saw his master on his knees doing such a humbling, selfless work, he refused to let Jesus wash his feet. Why? In Peter's mind, masters don't do such things. They don't abase themselves in such a manner as this. But this is where Jesus set the standard for service for anyone who looks to be in a high position. He told Peter that if He didn't wash his feet, then Peter would have no part in Him. In other words, there was no way Peter could ever be like Him. He would forfeit the right to the power, blessings, and relationship that comes from being in communion with Christ. What do you think would have happened if Jesus hadn't corrected Peter and he found himself in the position of being someone's master teacher later on? He would have been the type of leader that wouldn't allow himself to be vulnerable or humble. Sound familiar? When we refuse the work because we're more concerned about our name, we fail to represent Christ. This type of humility is needed for the church to unite and move forward as one unit.

It's not so much a problem when leaders come together in reaction to something that has already taken place and the church wants to confront it. Recently, in reaction to the violence of law enforcement officers against citizens, leaders have come together to take a stand and show some solidarity. In those situations, there was an immediate issue that had to be addressed right away. This type of action is absolutely necessary, but have you asked yourself why do we only come together in reaction to tragedies that have already occurred? What if we would try to get in front of these issues and attempt to prevent them from happening? Oh, we can come together to put on a conference or a concert, but what about catching these young men before they get caught up in the penal system? What about addressing teen pregnancy, which seems to be an issue nobody talks about anymore? Try to come together as one body and put together a strategy to tackle these issues and see who all will be on board after their name may not have been mentioned. This is another sad testimony against the church.

Why Unify?

You may be asking, what's the big deal anyway? People seem to be getting out of here going to heaven just fine with things the way they are now, so why mess up a good thing? (I'm being sarcastic.) The biggest reason why this is a big deal can be found in the 17th chapter of John where Jesus prayed to the Father that He would make us one as He and the Father are one, so the world may believe that He sent Jesus. This is a huge deal! Think about that last part for a second. Jesus prayed that the Father would make us one so people would believe. Our failure to come together as one body is keeping people from seeing Jesus and believing. This was more than just a prayer. It was part of the Lord's strategy for reaching the world.

Now, I could stop right there because for anyone who truly wants to see people in the world saved, that should be cause enough to unify. But there are other reasons as well, one of which is the economic power the church would have. Some churches are even afraid to talk about money let alone get to a point financially where it's not an issue. Our division keeps us from realizing the financial power we have in this world.

For example, in the Dallas/Ft. Worth Metroplex, there are about 3,000 churches. We did an extremely rough estimate once and found that if each of these churches had a membership of 100 people, with an average annual salary of $50K per member, and all of those members tithed, in a year's time there would be a total of about $1.6 billion dollars collected. Ask anyone who understands economics and they will tell you that whenever any group of people makes a billion dollars, you will command attention in any market. We take that same $1.6 billion and deposit it in banks that don't like to lend to churches. We take from the economy of the Kingdom and place our money in the world's economy. The same world that hates our Lord and His ways.

Why is this so important? The time is fast approaching where anyone that mentions the name of Jesus will risk losing their livelihood. It's already happening in some places. The world is slowly tightening its grip around the church's neck and threatening us that if we openly declare His name in any way, we will suffer. The church has to get to a place where it can sustain itself. Everything we need is in the body already so why does this threat impact us so greatly? It's because we're not unified enough to see that God has already provided.

I remember a friend calling me once and asking me if I knew a prayer that would fix finances. I laughed to myself and replied that I knew of no such prayer, and in case you're curious, no such prayer exists. I asked her where this was coming from. She began to tell me how financially things were a mess between her and her husband. I asked her if their finances were together and she said they weren't. I then saw the problem. Let's say she made $1,000 a month and her husband made the same. Their bills were $1,500 a month. Because they weren't united financially, she was looking at her $1,000 a month, then looking at the $1,500 in bills, and becoming frustrated because it didn't appear she had enough. Her husband was doing the exact same thing. If they had only united their finances, they would have looked at the bills from the perspective of having $2,000, and they wouldn't have looked liked they were more than they could handle. Thinking individually, they were stressed out and frustrated, but if they would only come together, they would see they had what they needed. The prayer had already been answered.

This is what goes on with the church. We can't see the forest for the trees. We look at the challenge of sustaining ourselves from the perspective of our own little church. If we would only come together, we would see that God has already given us what we need to break our dependency on the world. He said to owe no man nothing but love. We could do that and more if we would see that we are greater together than apart. People wouldn't have to worry about being fired from their job for taking a stand for Christ because the employer is a believer. We wouldn't have to worry about not qualifying for social programs because we don't agree with something we are required to in order to get funds and resources. The church would be able to fund its own programs. It's a sad thing that although we serve the God who owns everything, we live in fear that the world will one day cut us off.

This is just an example of what a unified church can accomplish. There are many others. If the church united, we could greatly reduce the amount of single parent homes in this nation. We could also put a huge dent in the number of teen pregnancies nationwide. We could greatly reduce the number of men that get locked up, and also drastically reduce recidivism, repeatedly going back to prison, because there would be hope in the world again. We could get more believers in public office. We could open and run more schools that teach what should be taught in schools. We could eliminate divorce among believers. Am I just dreaming? No, I just believe in the power of Christ working through a unified church. To echo the sentiment of John Lennon, you may say that I'm a dreamer, but I'm not the only one. Hopefully, one day you will join us, and the body of Christ will live as one.

CHAPTER 7

TITHING OPTIONAL?

BEFORE I WRAP THIS THING UP, I just have to touch on something that seems to be a tremendous challenge to people who attend church. This something is tithing. Tithing has become an ugly word to some people. People can be praising God like they've lost their mind, but as soon as you mention tithes and offering, you can feel the air get sucked out of the room. It's painful to watch pastors plead with people to pay tithes. They try encouragement, scare tactics, and even giving to congregants based on the promise that that person will pay tithes on what they receive, a priming of the pump if you will. All this is done in the effort to get people to pay tithes.

Why does it take so much to get someone to do something that is their duty as a believer to do? Even when God says that this is where we rob Him, we still fail to consistently pay tithes (Malachi 3:8). I hear some people saying, "Tithing was under the law, and we are no longer under the law. We are under grace." People who make statements like this are just looking for justification to not do something they don't want to do and try to make themselves feel better about doing wrong. Being under grace and not under the law means that you no longer need to be told what to do. You automatically do, or fulfill, the requirements of the law without constantly having to be reminded. That means that the pastor doesn't have to convince you to pay tithes. He doesn't have to pump and prime people who are under grace.

We have made tithing too much of an emotional thing. A lot of times in church we have to generate a feeling before we take up tithes and offering, and sadly enough, the collection plate becomes a gauge of how well you did at rousing the crowd. We have become a generation who only does things after you explain to us why we should do it. I can remember times when my mom would tell me to do something and if I asked why, she would simply say, "Because I said so!", and that would be the end of that. God operates a lot like that. He doesn't tell you why until you have obediently completed what He asked you to do. Does He really have to explain why first? If He is Lord, that means we don't debate Him on His word. We simply obey. What would happen to you if when your mom or dad told you to do something, you said to them, "I don't feel like it." Personally, I would have been picking my teeth up off the floor. What do you think God does when you tell Him you don't feel like doing what He said? I hear you..."I would never say that to God!" Do you realize that when you refuse to do what

He says, this is what your actions are saying to Him, and to His face no less? We sit back and wonder why things are not working in our lives and never consider what our actions have been saying to God. Shame on us!

Well, for those who need an explanation, if you will bear with me for a moment, I would like to bring a little understanding to this thing called tithing. Answer this for me, if Uncle Sam didn't take taxes out of your check automatically, would you voluntarily pay your taxes? And what would happen in this nation if paying taxes was a voluntary action? Crime would be out of control because there would be no law enforcement. Those who depend on government programs to feed their families and keep their health intact would starve and die. This nation would be open for any other country to take over us because there would be no armed forces for our defense. These are just a few things that this country would suffer through, and all because you decided not to pay taxes.

The tithe is a tax. It's the way we fund the things needed to maintain the work the Kingdom is responsible for, and because we take our tithes and give them to the world, believers have to depend on the world to make certain their needs are met. This makes God look like He's not able to take care of His people, which causes people not to believe in Jesus Christ. The Kingdom of God has an economic system that is being bankrupted by God's people because we refuse to pay into the system.

Yes, the United States is a government, but in case you didn't know, so is the Kingdom. A kingdom is a form of government headed by a King. Jesus Christ is the King. King is a governmental leadership position, not a church leadership position. He is the leader of our government, and His government has everything we need. As a believer, you are a citizen of the Kingdom of Heaven.

If you understand citizenship, you know that there are certain rights and privileges afforded to you by simply being a citizen. Those rights and privileges are available to those in right standing with the government. That means you are a law-abiding citizen. This right standing with the law is called righteousness. Jesus told us to seek first the Kingdom and its righteousness, then all these will be added. If we would simply get this revelation, a lot of what we read in the Bible, and the things Christ said to us would make a lot of sense, including tithes.

You can't claim to belong to Christ and His Kingdom nor claim you're righteous if you don't pay tithes. In the United States, there is a push to make the undocumented workers citizens. It has been the source of much controversy, but why do you think they want to rush to make them citizens? It's so they can tax them! Because they're not citizens, they use the resources of this nation and are not giving back. We do the same thing when we don't pay tithes. On the other hand, they don't have access to the benefits that come with citizenship either. Many of us feel we have access to Kingdom benefits, but we won't fulfill the righteous requirement of the law as it pertains to tithes.

That's just the tithe. There's still a matter of the offering. As many of you know, the offering is what you give over and above the tithe. For instance, if you decide to give twelve percent of your income, only two percent of that twelve percent would be your offering or seed. So if you make $100k a year and you give $12K to your church, only $2,000 of that will be your seed. So don't the mistake of thinking that all the money you give is seed money.

There are people that believe you get blessed off of the tithe. This is false information. It's become common in this nation for people to want special credit for doing what they're supposed to do anyway. If part of your chores as a child was to clean up your room, and you did just that, you didn't get special privileges for doing so. It was part of your duties as a member of the household. Now, if you decided to clean your room, the kitchen, and the bathroom as well, your parents may give you a little extra in your allowance or take you to McDonald's and get you a real meal instead of those little happy meals. This is special rewards or privileges for giving of your own free will to do more than what was required of you. This is how offering works.

Looking at that same scenario, if you cleaned the kitchen and bathroom, but neglected your regular duty of cleaning your room, you wouldn't get the special privileges and rewards you may have thought you would. Why, because you didn't fulfill the basic requirement. Many of us do extra things that are good, but neglect to do what's right. That goes for tithes & offering and everything else. Dr. Munroe used to say, "The enemy of right things is often good things." Someone might say they decided to give their money to a homeless shelter rather than pay tithes. Yes, they did a good thing, but it wasn't the right thing. If you fulfill your duties consistently and pay your tithes, and have a heart to do more, God may give you increase to do the extra that's in your heart to do. The increase may not be in the form of money, but rather an opportunity like a promotion at your job or a business venture that will add to you.

The thing to remember is that God is the source. As a Kingdom citizen, you must operate with that understanding. Your job is not your source. Neither is mom or dad. They are resources. If you understand resources, you know they are limited. Your job may close its doors and mom or dad may go bankrupt, but your provision didn't dry up with their inability to provide. God can always provide another resource. Your access to that resource depends on you properly handling what God has placed in your hands.

Another thing to make special note of is that it all belongs to God anyway. You may think that after you've given your tithe, the ninety percent left is yours, but that's not true. The whole one hundred percent is His. God is not looking for people He can get things to. He's looking for people He can get things through. The tithe is for operation and maintenance of the Kingdom. The ninety percent is for you to establish yourself in the assignment He's given you specifically. It's to help you be independent (demonstrating responsibility) and to eventually establish yourself as a resource. The Bible says in Psalm 1:3 that you shall be, "...like a tree planted by rivers of water..." Rivers indicate something flowing, let's say money for instance. We want the flow to stop at us. A tree planted by a flowing river benefits from the flow of the river. It doesn't have to be in the flow directly, although that's where we want to be. A tree in the river can block the flow. Rivers give. Reservoirs receive.

God always referred to rivers when He talks to us. If God knows He can get it through you, He will make sure to get it to you. We are blessed to be a blessing. That's why the Bible says it's more blessed to give than to receive. When you understand that God owns it all, as you're going about your day, He can say to you at any time, "Release $100 to the lady that works across the hall from you." If you think it's yours, you will start to debate with God about "your" money. Eventually, you miss an opportunity to be used by God and bless someone in need, and you also show God that He cannot get it through you. In nature, if a river's flow gets blocked, the water will find another way through. The water takes the "path of least resistance"! God does the same thing. He finds the person who won't put up a fight on releasing His resources where He needs them to. That person is the one that will be blessed continually.

And another thing, if you won't pay tithes in your local church because you feel the pastor is stealing money and you can't trust him, you need to find another church with a pastor you can trust. God will not accept that excuse. Why take the chance on missing out on the rights and privileges of the Kingdom all because you decided your pastor was a crook and you weren't giving him any of your money? When you give your tithes and offerings, you are not giving to the pastor. You are giving to the church, the body of Christ. If your pastor is stealing, let God deal with him on that. The thing for you to do is stop calling him your pastor and find another body to connect with that does the work Christ requires us to do.

I hope this has helped someone in their understanding of tithes and offerings. The important thing to keep in mind is that it always begins with obedience. Worry about the why later. God is not trying to keep His ways and plans from us. He wants us to know them, but most importantly, He wants us to be an active participant in establishing His Kingdom on the earth. So, let's seek first the Kingdom. That means we look to do what is first going to benefit the Kingdom. Then, let's establish ourselves in righteousness, which means doing things His way. If we do, God will fulfill His word to us and add "all these things".

CHAPTER 8

CULTURE IS KEY

SO, WHAT'S THE CONCLUSION OF THE MATTER? How do we get back to an effective form of Christianity? What has to happen for us to truly begin to impact the world the way Jesus Christ intended for us to? What is it going to take to begin to alleviate these things that seem so minute, but are truly keeping the church from coming together and reaching a dying world?

One thing we have to understand is that the setup of this country as it pertains to religion has damaged our mindsets. We compartmentalize church in our lives and it becomes just something we do like going to the gym or the grocery store. It's just something we fit in. Our belief in Christ doesn't seem to encompass our entire lives. We tend to take an "Oh, by the way" attitude when it comes to living according to word of God. We never seem to adopt living for Christ as a way of life.

My wife and I had our honeymoon in Mexico. We didn't go on a cruise, rather we stayed at a resort in Mexico. Therefore, it wasn't an American trip with a taste of Mexico. It was all Mexico all the time. Spanish is the primary language with a few people speaking English. When we watched television, it was all Spanish with English subtitles. We had to convert our money into pesos, or at least understand the exchange rate. Needless to say, we were submerged in the Mexican culture.

We were there for an entire week, absorbing the language, tasting the food, encountering the people, and pretty much living according to the Mexican customs and way of life. When we returned home, while we were out at restaurants, as our waiter or waitress would serve us, we would say "Gracias" as we were being served and "Si" whenever they asked us a question. Although we had returned home to America and American customs, we were still in a Mexico state of mind subconsciously. Mexico had gotten into our hearts. I'm not saying we fell in love with Mexico. I'm saying after being submerged in their culture for only a week, their language had leaked into our subconscious mind.

I just emphasized "submerged" for a reason. Think for a moment. What happens when you are baptized? You are submerged into the water. Yes, I know that some people sprinkle, which is something I disagree with and I think you'll understand why once I finish my explanation. The submerging you go through during baptism is symbolic, much like the crackers and wine are symbolic of Jesus' broken body and blood in communion. You don't really drink His blood and eat His body. In the same regard, that water does not change you. It is a representation of the change that is taking place in you. Just like my wife and I were submerged into the Mexican culture, your submersion into the water during baptism is supposed to represent your submersion into Christ and living for Christ.

In Acts 17:28, the Bible says, "For in Him we live and move and have our being...", which is to say we should be totally submerged in to His life and lifestyle. That means there has to be a culture present that completely represents Christ and His life. One that we can get submerged into like my wife and I in Mexico. That's true baptism. It's going all the way in, not being sprinkled with Christ on just a part of your body. Your whole entire being has to be in Him. That's the only way to be completely affected by Christ to the point where we change not only our clothes, but our hearts as well.

When John the Baptist was baptizing in the wilderness, he wouldn't even baptize a person unless they showed signs of repentance. There would have to be clear signs that they had changed before he would dip them into the water. Now, I didn't say remorse, which is what most of us show in church. Remorse is feeling sorry or expressing regret for something you've done. Repenting is completely changing your mind and turning away from the pattern of thinking that lead you to the act for which you are showing remorse. I have to stress this. Repenting is not you telling God you're sorry for the wrong you've done and asking Him to forgive you. It's completely acknowledging that your "stinking thinking" got you in the mess you were in and that in order to truly stay away from that behavior you must adopt His way of thinking and being.

The problem with believers in this nation is that we bring our cultures into the church rather than adopting the Kingdom culture set up for us by the King, Jesus Christ. Well, that's because there really isn't a place where we can go to submerge ourselves in the Kingdom lifestyle. We have been in our worldly cultures our entire lives and just having a Sunday morning experience is not powerful enough to uproot the old culture of our heart (subconscious mind) and replace it with Christ. There has to be more. That's why we must read our Bibles daily and pray without ceasing. It's how we submerge ourselves.

The Bible says we live by faith and that faith comes by our hearing, or rather what we hear the most. It's a natural principle that whatever you listen to, or hear, the most you develop faith in. If a child constantly hears from their parents that they are bad, eventually they will develop faith in that and act according to that faith. When you read your Bible, you are hearing God's word. When you pray without ceasing, you are rehearsing, or re-hearing, His word. You have to flood your hearing with God's word, whether it be reading His word, praying, talking about Him with other believers, or listening to sound teaching on Him and His Kingdom as you go about your day.

One of the most powerful statements I have ever heard came from Dr. Munroe. He said, "Culture is stronger than law." That may not mean much to you, but you have wondered why people in church, regardless of what's being taught, still seem to get caught up in the same things the world does. We still struggle with divorce in the church. We battle with teen pregnancy in the church. Adultery and fornication are still a problem in the church. Why do these worldly issues prevail in the place where God says that these things should not be named among us? It's because these problems still exist in the cultures we still live in while we tell ourselves we are in this world, but not of this world.

People do not follow law. They follow culture. People do not do what the law says. They do what they see people doing. This is the problem with the church. Too many new believers see people living lives contradictory to God's word. When they come into the church and see people who they believe have been walking with God longer, doing things that are wrong, they believe that's the way things should be done. The current church culture promotes putting on a facade so everything looks fine in your life although it's not. People don't really see that God still holds us accountable for living according to His word. They don't get to see the whipping God has to put on us for doing wrong. This is one of the evils under the sun like Solomon mentioned.

When the culture agrees with the law, people live right. All that has been mentioned in this book has been to make us aware of the current culture that exists in many churches and how that culture doesn't agree with God's intentions. The Kingdom has its own culture that we can and should adopt into our lives. That culture agrees with the King and His will. It's time that we begin to live according to life in the Kingdom of God. When we do this, our Christianity will become effective in winning souls, living truly prosperous lives, and establishing Christ's Kingdom in the earth. I pray this read has blessed you.

About the Author

Growing up in Bastrop, a small city in northeast Louisiana, Derrick Smith was no stranger to church. His mother was heavily involved in church life in the area, so she assured that his involvement would be significant as well. Early in his teenage years, he held several positions in his home church including assistant secretary, steward (Methodist church), and usher. Needless to say, Derrick was indoctrinated into church culture early in life, and developed a love for it and what it stood for, but he could not deny the contradictions in what he heard from the pulpit versus what he witnessed in the communities around him.

After graduating from Grambling State University, Derrick moved to Plano, TX where he met his lovely wife, Salena, who happened to be the daughter of the pastor he would serve under. It was here that he would begin his journey to discover the source of the contradictions he saw both back home in Louisiana and even in his new home in Texas. Where was the power the church was supposed to have? What was blocking it? These are questions he sought God for answers to.

In 2006, he began studying the Kingdom of God and gained perspective on the issues plaguing the church today. Although the issues run pretty deep, Derrick wanted to address some of the simple things that rob the church of its power today. As The Bible says, it's the small foxes that destroy the vine. This particular body of work addresses the simple things that may otherwise be overlooked, but can cause a fair amount of damage to the Body of Christ. He has a heart to see the church become the powerful entity God intended from the beginning. This book is his contribution to helping God's will be realized today. Thank you for reading!

Acknowledgments

At this time, I would like to thank for all the women in my life (fellas, I'll get you on the next book). First, to the best mother to ever walk God's green earth, Ernestine Smith. Thank you for the foundation you gave me in Christ. You trained me well and I did not depart. Rest on, mama.

To the love of my life, my best friend, my good thing, my wife Salena, thank you for putting up with me. You're the driving force behind all I aspire to achieve. I love you with everything in me!

To all my sisters, Monica, Debbie, Rosalind, San, Mary, and Jo (God rest), I thank God for all of you. I know I'm horrible about keeping in touch, but never doubt the fact that I love you guys.

To all my nieces (that's a lot of names, ladies), I love all of you and wish nothing but God's best for all of you!

To my mother-n-law and sisters-n-law, that you for adding to the wealth of amazing women in my life, and for welcoming me into your family. I love you guys.

www.ingramcontent.com/pod-product-compliance
Lightning Source LLC
Chambersburg PA
CBHW051847040426
42447CB00006B/729